Early-Level Classics

CORNELIUS GURLITT

LATE-ELEMENTARY PIANO SOLOS

BOOK 1

Little Melodic Études

Opus 187

EDITED BY GAIL LEW

PREFACE

Book 1 contains 54 relatively short character études from Opus 187 that are important for the development of technic, independence of the hands, and the playing of passagework for the young pianist. The pieces contain familiar patterns that fit well under the small hand and are highly idiomatic to the romantic period.

Gurlitt became the chief organist of his native town in Altona, Germany, and one of the later nineteenth century's most prodigious providers of well-graded piano music. His music continues to be taught in countries around the world.

The pieces are all short because lengthy pieces easily overwhelm the capacity and the patience of the beginning student. In most of these pieces, no interval larger than a fifth is used, which allows the student to keep his or her eyes on the musical score. Both homophonic and polyphonic writing for the keyboard are featured in this collection, and both hands learn automatically to work independently of each other. In some pieces Gurlitt gives the melody to either the right hand or the left hand, with a softer accompaniment in the other hand. Each piece is short—often eight or sixteen measures—and rhythm and time signatures have been varied. The student is advised to read through each part separately and then, when each part is mastered, play both parts together at a very slow tempo, gradually increasing the tempo. For advanced students, these pieces may also be recommended both as exercises in sight playing and as materials for the study and practice of transposition.

Gail Lew

Cover Design: Marco Brandão
Production Coordinator: Sheryl Rose

ABOUT THE EDITOR

Gail Lew is the director of keyboard publications for Warner Bros. Publications in Miami, Florida. Gail has served as senior piano editor for Kjos Music in San Diego, new music reviewer for the *California Music Teacher* magazine, and clinician for Frederick Harris Music Company in Toronto. She received her bachelor of music degree in piano performance and continued her graduate studies in music education and music history and literature. Following graduate school, Gail pursued a career as a private piano instructor. She conducts yearly workshops in the United States and Canada, including presentations at the Music Teachers National Association Convention, many of its state affiliates, and the World Piano Pedagogy Conference.

Gail has received national acclaim for her carefully edited and researched editions of music by Alexandre Tansman, Dmitri Kabalevsky, Samuel Maykapar, Darius Milhaud, Yoshinao Nakada, Robert Starer, and Alexander Tcherepnin. She has also compiled technic studies for the popular series ***Technic Is Fun*** and written arrangements of popular music for the new ***Looney Tunes Piano Library***, an educational supplemental library of piano music written specifically to correlate with all piano methods.

PERFORMANCE NOTES

As soon as the beginning pianist is able to play each of the pieces easily, he or she is ready to transpose them to different keys. Études Nos. 1–12 are performed one octave apart. They have been purposely engraved two octaves apart with an *8va* indication allowing students to read right hand in treble clef and left hand in bass clef. The unison playing in Nos. 1–10 will allow students to be carefully and continually aware of the touch, and with the body, the elbows, the wrists, and the fingers kept in proper positions. The student may also use this collection of pieces to advantage by counting the beats aloud and steadily. It is suggested that the student warm up by playing a major five-finger pattern and broken chord several times in the key of each piece.

Example in C Major (transpose to other keys):

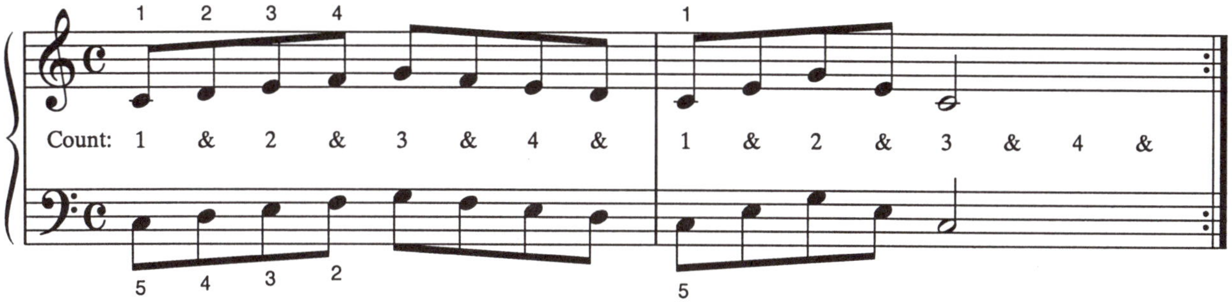

Dynamic signs of expression, such as ***f***, ***p***, *crescendo,* and so on, were purposely omitted by the composer in Nos. 1–22. The études, however, are easy enough for the student to focus on tone production, connection of the tones *(legato),* and acquiring a *cantabile* (singing) style.

Every piano teacher who has taught beginners knows that any beginning is difficult. In this area the great masters have left little or nothing for students. The present work, therefore, aims, within its self-elected limits, to help fulfill this need. Nothing larger than the interval of a fifth is used in Nos. 1–31, so the student has no reason to look away from the music at the keys. The eye thus accustoms itself to the significance of the notation, mechanical playing by heart is avoided, and the student learns to "read." At the same time, care is taken to offer no difficulty that the student is not able to master before becoming too familiar with his or her piece. Velocity is in no case necessary in these exercises. In études Nos. 1–31, the performer may choose his or her tempo. The composer indicated tempo markings only in études Nos. 32–54.

Beginning in exercise No. 7, the student begins to develop independence of the hands. Melodic lines will alternate between right hand and left hand, and some of the studies use both parallel and contrary motion. This type of writing prepares the sutdent for the polyphonic style of the early masters.

(performance notes continued on page 4)

PERFORMANCE NOTES (continued from page 3)

Nos. 1–20
Strive for a continuous *legato* touch throughout the entire piece. The composer purposely left dynamics to the discretion of the performer. Practice each étude using different dynamic levels. Vary the dynamics between left hand and right hand by playing left hand *forte* and right hand *mezzo forte.* Then reverse the dynamics by playing left hand *mezzo forte* and right hand *forte.* These exercises may also be practiced with left hand *staccato* and right hand *legato* followed by left hand *legato* and right hand *staccato.* Always maintain a steady beat.

No. 13
Play the right hand *mezzo forte* and the left hand accompaniment *mezzo piano* in this étude. The dynamics here are editorial and may be changed to right hand *forte* and left hand *mezzo forte* or right hand *mezzo piano* and left hand *piano.* The melody must always sing out above the left-hand accompaniment.

No. 14
The left-hand melody must be brought out and the right-hand accompaniment must be subdued in this short étude. The editorial suggestion is to play the right hand *mezzo piano* and the left hand *mezzo forte.*

Nos. 15–20
The composer left dynamics to the discretion of the performer in all of these pieces. Vary the pieces by using *staccato* and *legato* touches. Mark phrasing in the music.

Nos. 21–23
Each of these pieces works on balance between melody and accompaniment. The melody alternates between right and left hand. Mark where the melody goes and play only that melodic line, and then add the accompaniment.

Nos. 24–30
Follow the same performance suggestions used in Nos. 1–20 with regard to dynamics and articulation.

No. 31
Find the measures that are repeated in this piece. What dynamic changes would make these measures more interesting? Try different dynamic levels.

No. 32–36
Gurlitt indicates specific tempos, dynamics, and phrasing offering more challenges for the performer. Hand positions change continually, so each hand should be practiced separately.

No. 37
This piece is made up of broken chords. Try playing these chords as block chords. Write down the chord names. Keep the line moving so there is one continuous sweeping motion and the change from left hand to right hand will not be discernable. Pedal indications are editorial but will help accentuate the harmonic changes.

No. 38
Notice the long ties and be careful to hold these notes while playing the inner voices.

No. 39
Block the left-hand chords and identify the chords used. Find all the tonic and dominant chords. Play the left hand *legato* quietly in the background.

No. 40
Bring out the left-hand melody in this étude. Find the measures where the hand position changes. Keep a steady beat especially when the hand position changes. Mark all of these changes in the music. The composer marked this piece *piano.* Find appropriate places to add *crescendo* and *diminuendo.*

(performance notes continued on page 48)

CORNELIUS GURLITT
1820–1901

Cornelius Gurlitt was born February 10, 1820, in the city of Altona, Germany. He studied piano with the famous head of the Leipzig Conservatory, Johann Peter Reinecke, father of Carl Reinecke, where both he and the young Reinecke were classmates. His first public performance was at the age of seventeen. The gratifying reception he received prompted his move to Denmark to further his studies.

Upon receiving a royal Danish scholarship, Gurlitt continued his studies in organ, piano, and composition at the School of Music in Copenhagen with Christoph Ernst Friedrich Weyse. He became friends with the Norwegian composer Niels W. Gade during this time. In 1842 Gurlitt settled in Hirschholm, near Copenhagen, where he lived for four years. He then returned to Leipzig where Gade was director of the Gewandhaus concerts. In 1849 he became a military bandmaster and also served as an army conductor.

Before returning to Germany, Gurlitt went to Rome to visit his brother, Louis Gurlitt, a well-known landscape painter. The music of Gurlitt was already recognized for its musical merits, and the papal academy Di Santa Cecilia nominated him an honorary member and graduated him professor of music in 1855. Upon his return to Altona (which lies near Hamburg), he became an organist at the main church. He was also a teacher at the Hamburg Conservatory. In 1874 he became Royal Prussian Musikdirektor (director of a musical society). The Duke of Augustenburg engaged Gurlitt, now a much celebrated teacher, as teacher to three of his daughters.

Gurlitt belonged to the circle of friends of Robert Schumann and Johannes Brahms. One of his European concert tours included performances with Schumann and Franz Liszt. His compositions are prodigious in quantity. He composed two operas, three violin sonatas, three cello sonatas, and several song cycles, but he is primarily known for his numerous Schumannesque works for piano. He died in Altona, June 17, 1901.

Little Melodic Études

Opus 187

CORNELIUS GURLITT

1

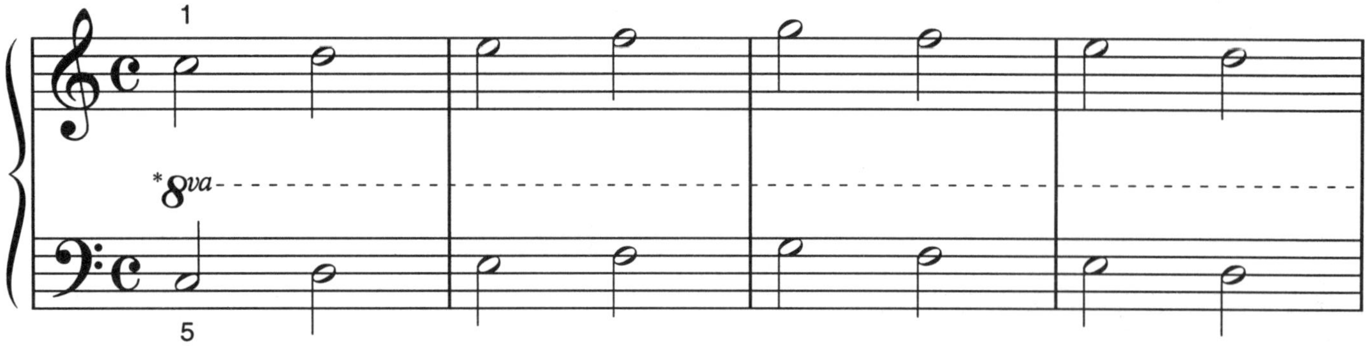

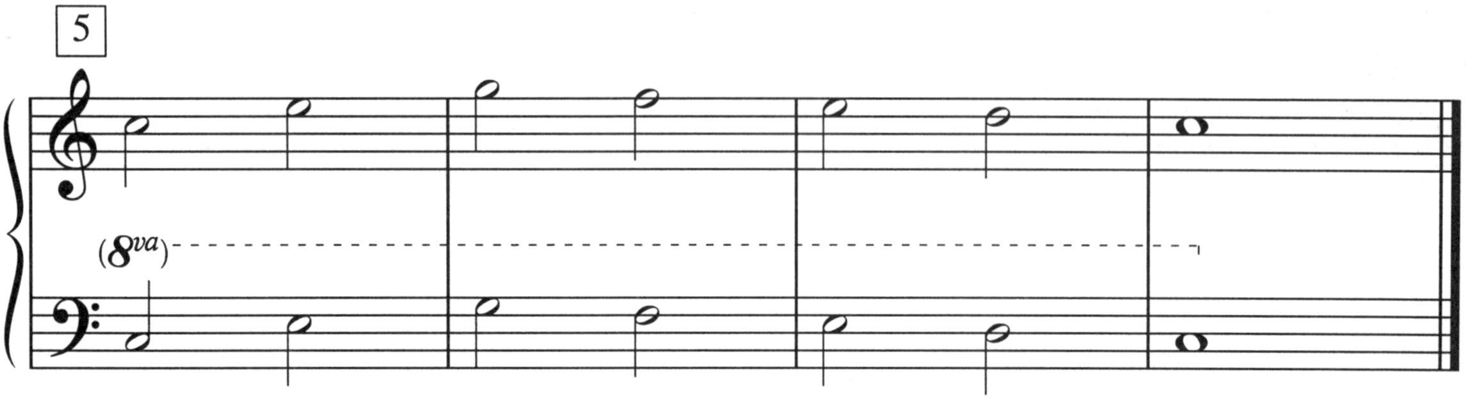

2

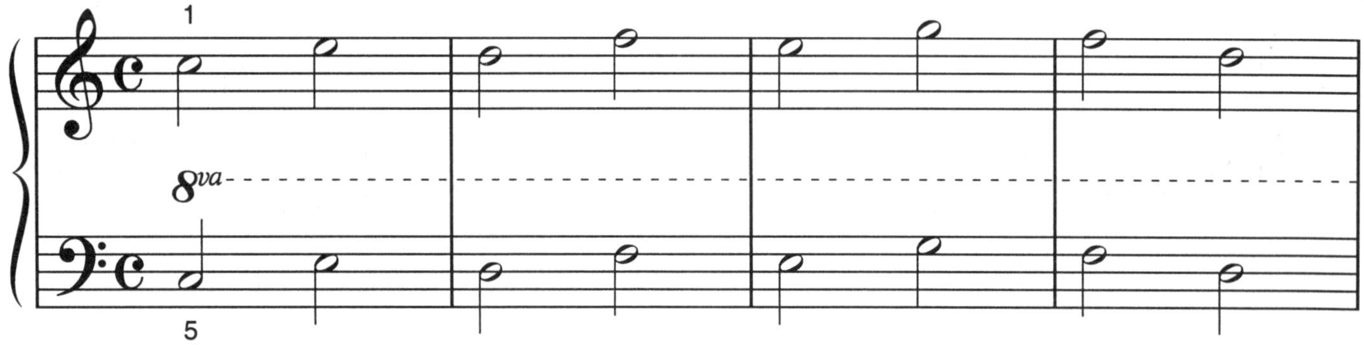

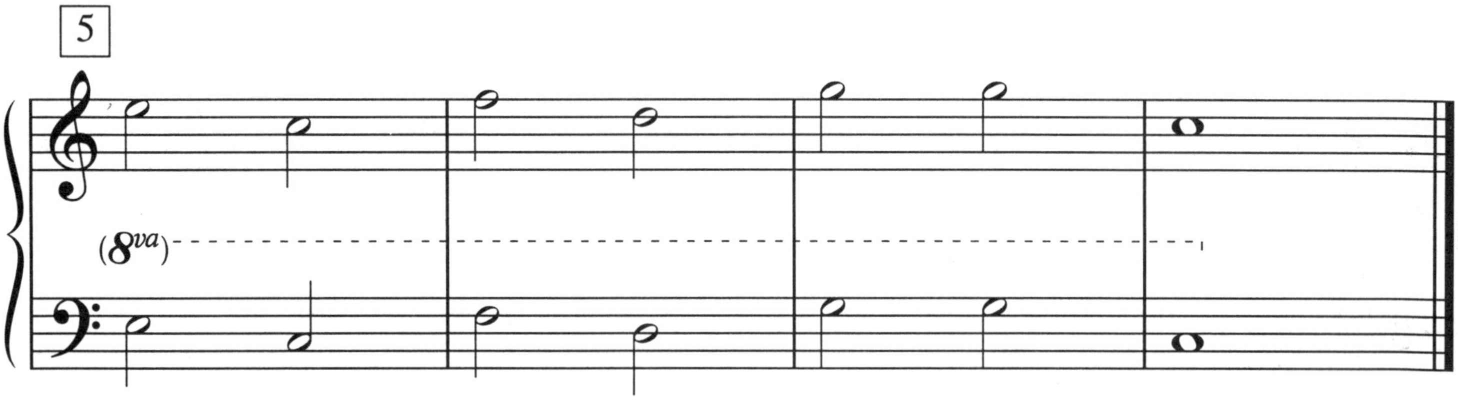

*Gurlitt wrote both right hand and left hand in treble clef. The decision to engrave left hand in the bass clef using an 8va sign in Nos. 1 - 12 was editorial. The composer did not indicate dynamic markings in Nos. 1 - 22.

1
3
8va
5
5
(8va)
1
4
8va
5
5
(8va)

5

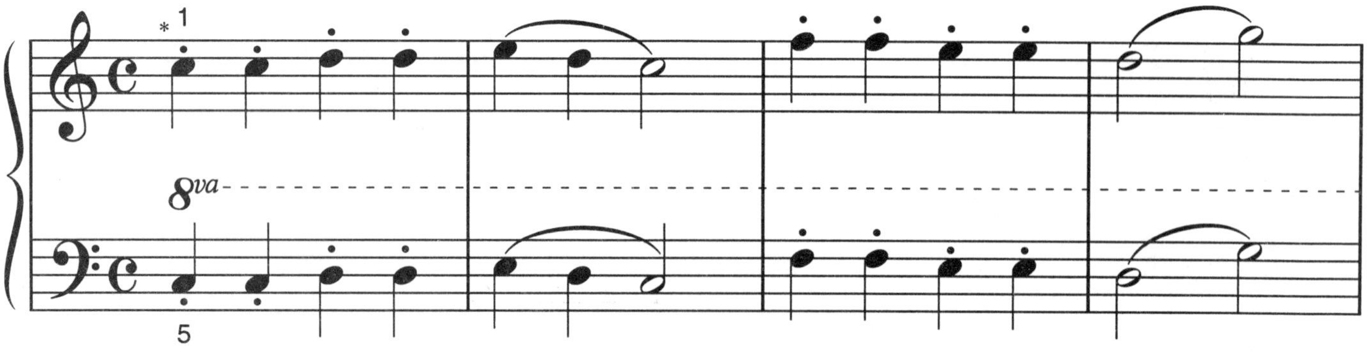

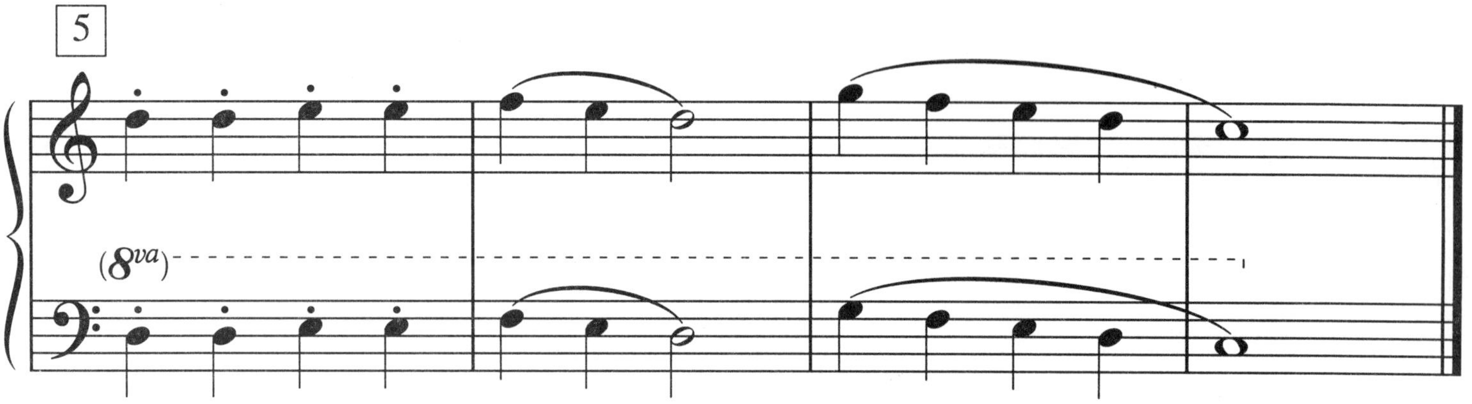

6

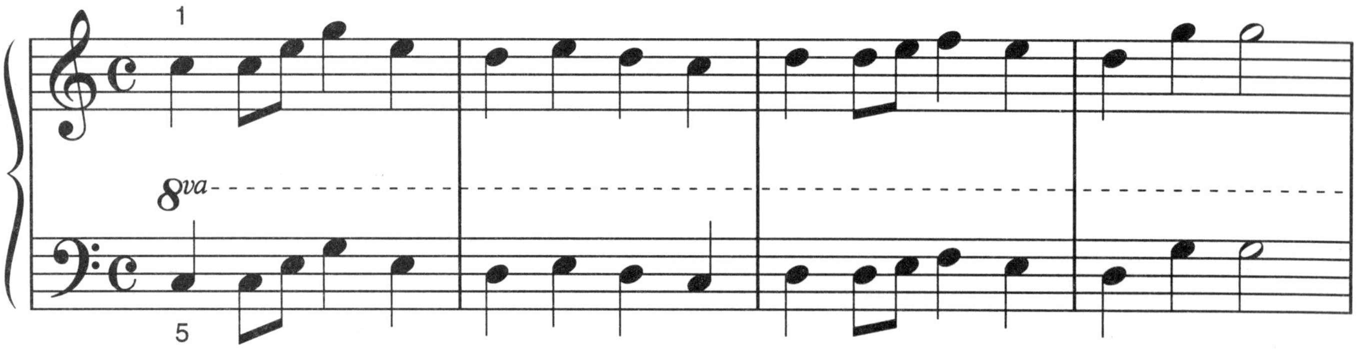

*Phrase markings and staccato indications are editorial.

7

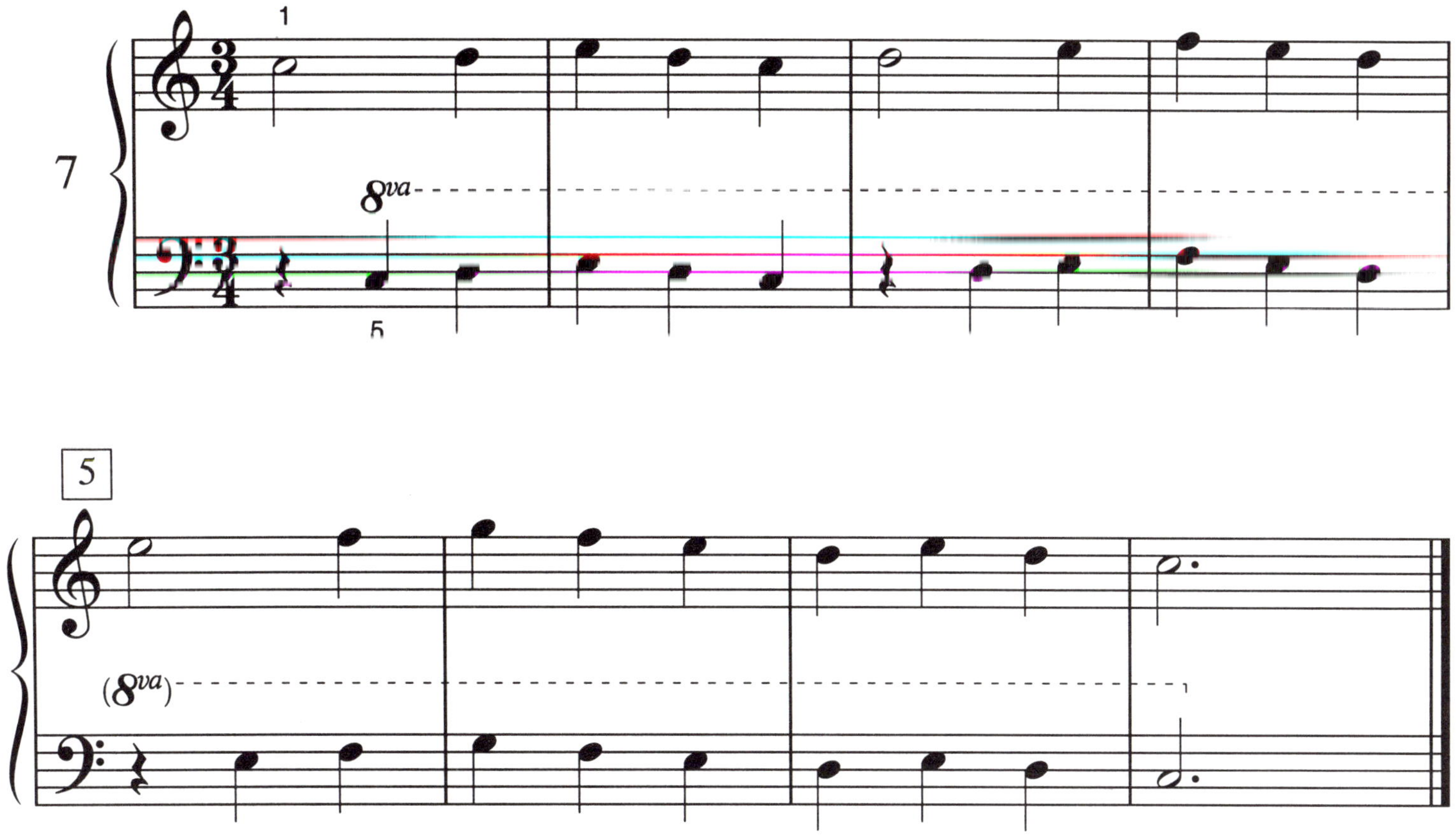

8

9

10

11
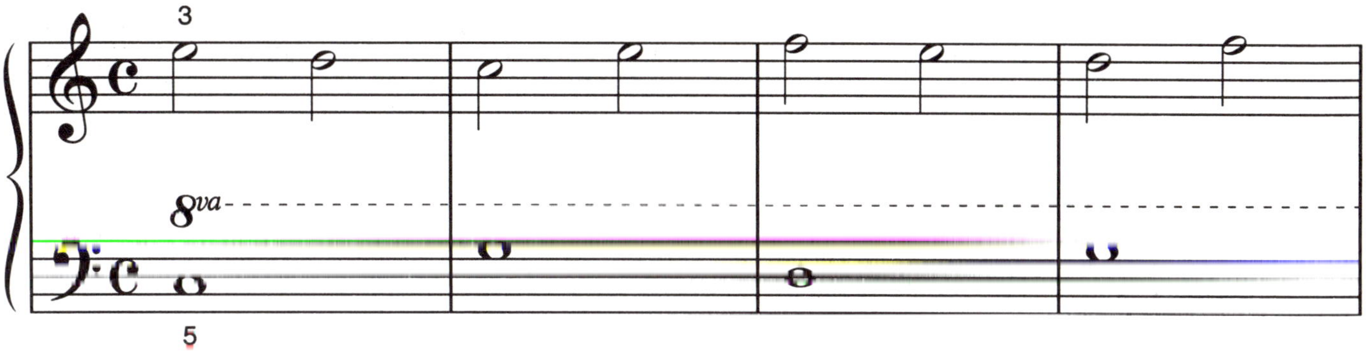

12
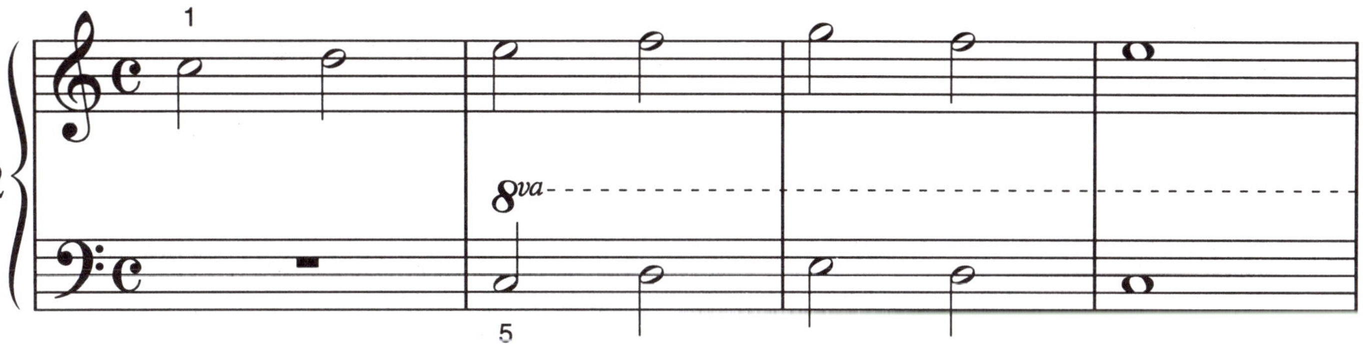

13

14

*Dynamic markings are editorial.

15

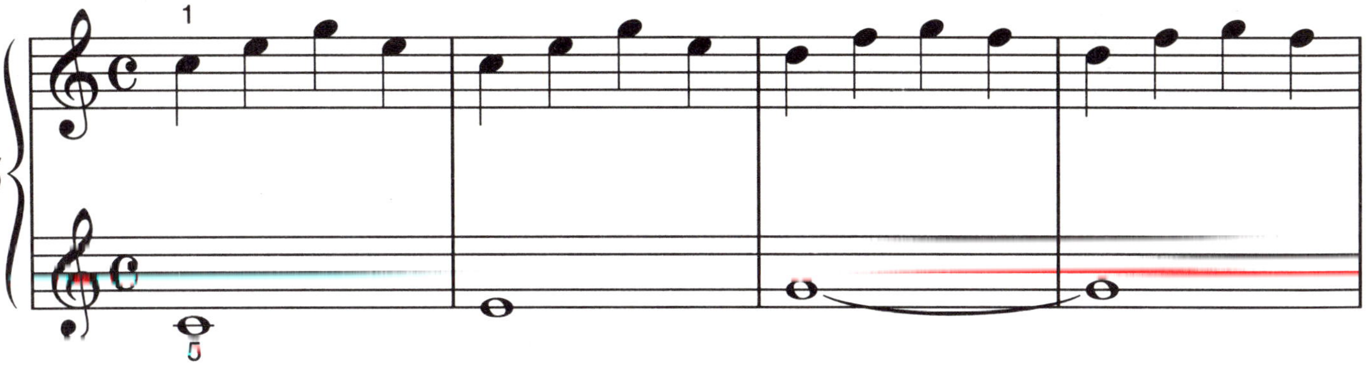

16

17

18

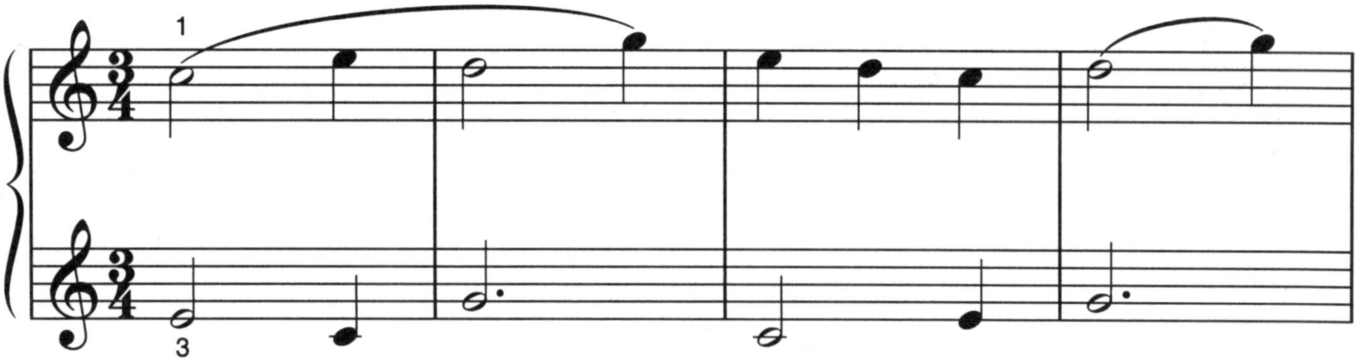

19
5
20
5

Music Box*

*The dynamic markings and title are editorial.

*The dynamic markings are editorial.

German Dance*

*This title is editorial.
**Dynamic markings are those of the composer.

24

25

26

27

28

29

30

31

*Phrase marks are editorial.

*Phrase marks in measures 6 and 7 are editorial. The suggested phrasing maintains consistency with the composer's own indications in measures 14 and 15.

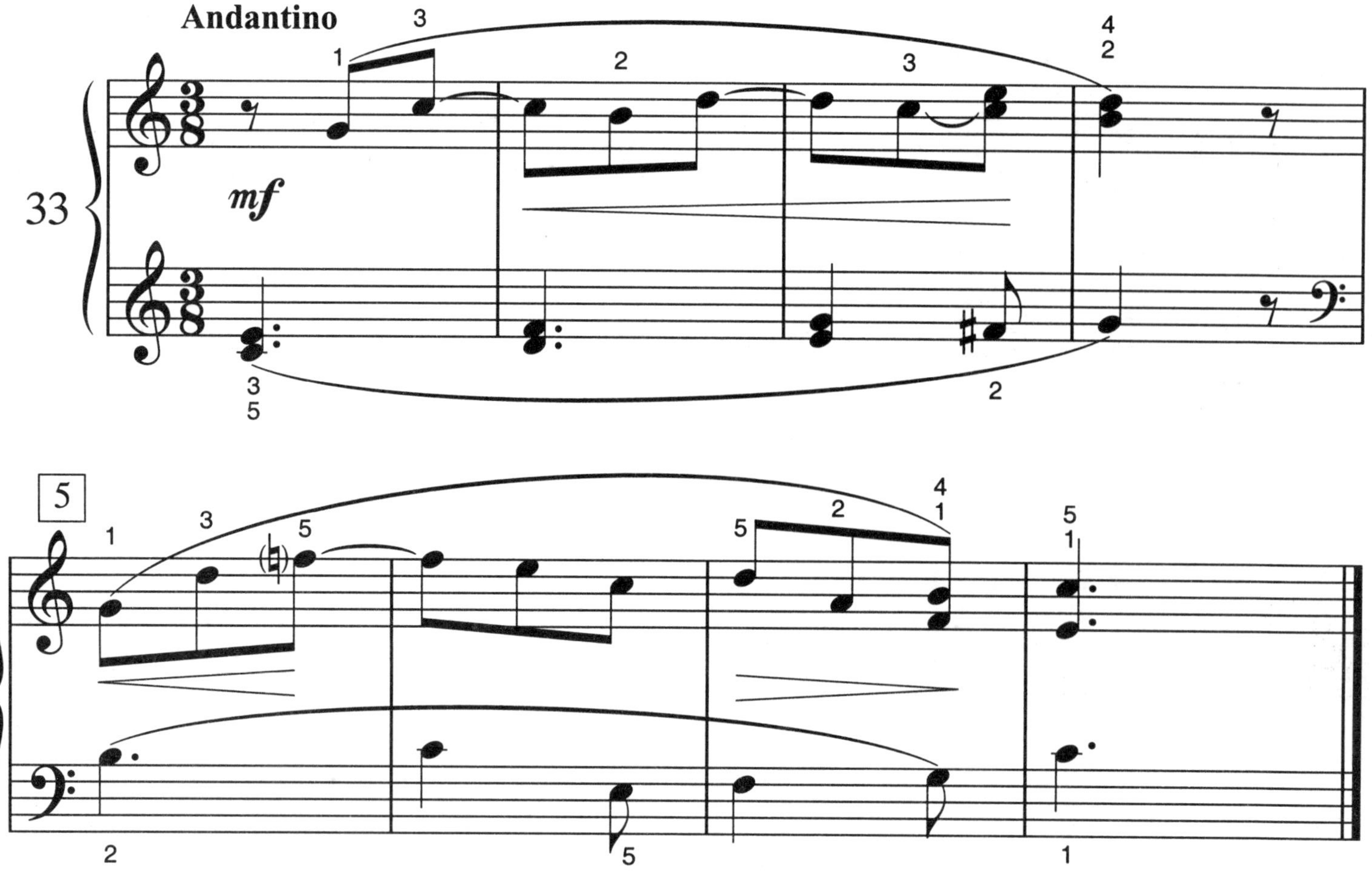

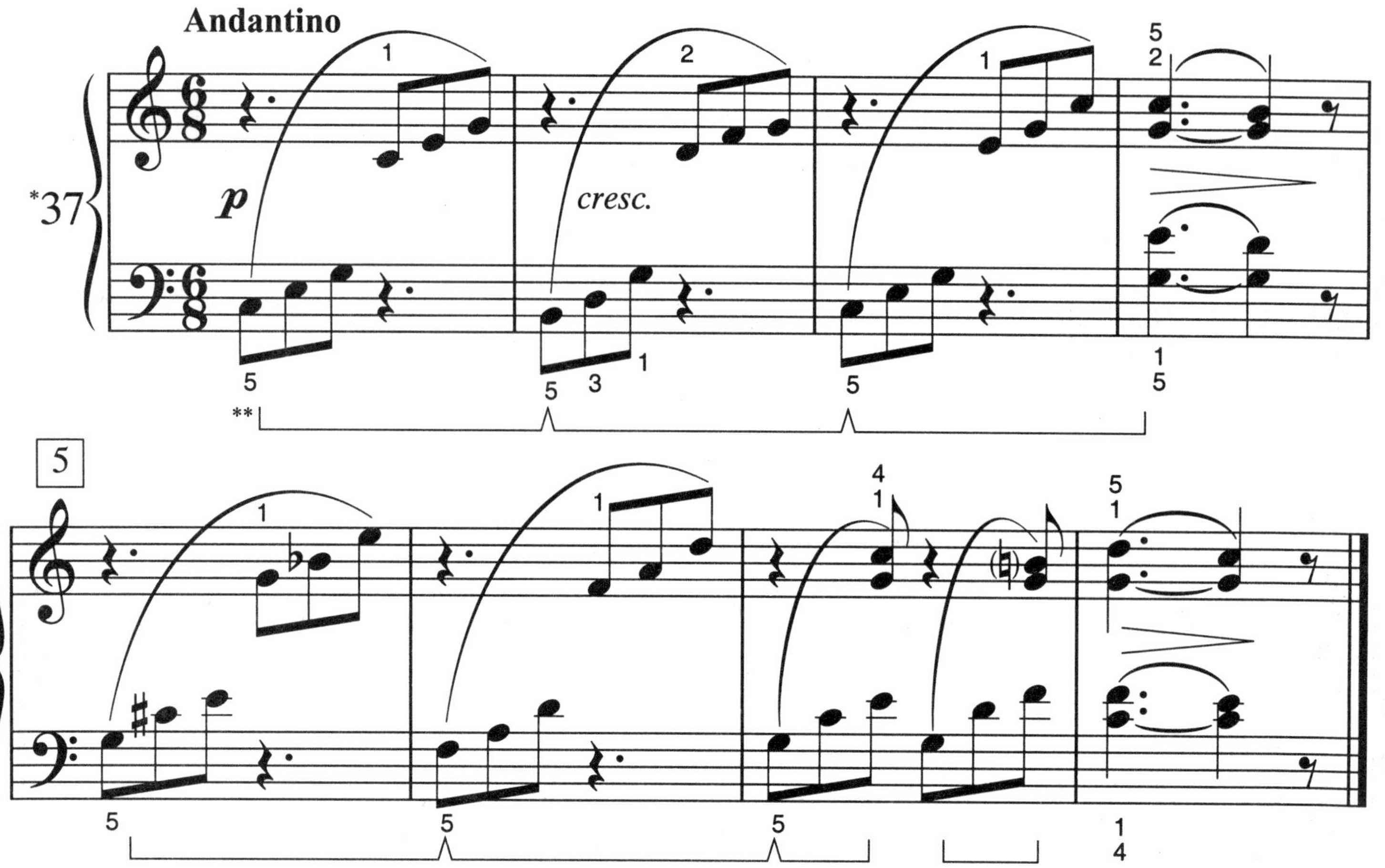

*Piano Solo No. 37 was placed out of numerical order to avoid awkward page turns.

**Pedal indications are editorial.

Little Waltz*

Tempo di valse

31

*This title is editorial. Gurlitt did not include titles for Opus 187.

Scherzo*

Moderato

*This title is editorial.

*Dynamic markings ***mf*** and ***p*** are editorial.

Con moto
38
p
5
9
13

Sonatina*

*This title is editorial.

Waltz*

*This title is editorial.

17
21
25
cresc.
29
dim.

Horn Call*

*This title is editorial.

9
cresc.
11
ff
f
13
15

Melody*

*This title is editorial.

**Melody (Piano Solo No. 41) was placed out of numerical order to avoid awkward page turns.

Little Mazurka*

*This title is editorial.

Moderato
44
f
mf
f

*Pedal indications are editorial.

Quiet Stream*

*This title is editorial.
**Pedal indications are editorial.

Mazurka*

Moderato

*This title is editorial.

Pastorale*

*This title is editorial.

Allegretto
49
mf
5
sf
9
13

Toccata*

*The title is editorial.
**Staccato markings in measures 6 and 8 are editorial.

Andantino
51
p
5
9
13

Impromptu*

*Pedal indications and title are editorial.

The Wanderer*

53

Allegretto

*This title is editorial.

Etude in F*

Moderato

*Pedal indications, title, and dynamic markings in measures 5, 7, 21, and 22 are editorial.

13
16
p
19
22

PERFORMANCE NOTES (continued from page 4)

No. 41
Even though this piece has a constantly moving eighth-note pattern, notice the up stems indicating quarter notes. Hold these notes for their full value and place slight emphasis on these notes to bring out a singing melodic line.

No. 42
Accentuate the two-note phrases by a slight crescendo. Keep the left hand eighth-note pattern connected and even.

No. 43
Carefully count the dotted rhythm and lift the hand at the end of the three-note phrases to give this étude a dance quality. Most mazurkas have dotted rhythms, syncopation, and stress on the second or third beat. Find those elements in this piece and mark places that would receive extra emphasis. Keep the tempo lively.

No. 44
The dynamics given are those of the composer. Be your own editor and try using different dynamic levels. Mark themes A and B in the music. Decide if the A theme should always be the same dynamic level.

No. 45
The broken chord melody must move smoothly between the left hand and right hand. Block the chords and notice how many times the C-major triad is used. Play the last four measures *pianissimo* and add a *ritardando.* Pedal indications are editorial.

No. 46
The broken chord melody in the right hand must be *sempre legato.* Block the chords and write the names of the chords used. The dynamics are those of the composer. He wants this piece to be quiet and tranquil.

No. 47
Although the title is editorial, this piece is definitely another mazurka. The composer indicates two-note phrases here. Dynamics were not given in measure 1, but the editor suggests beginning *mezzo piano.* Gurlitt indicates *forte* in measure 8 followed by a *diminuendo.*

No. 48–49
The composer offers only a few dynamic suggestions in these études. Additional dynamics could be added effectively, especially in No. 49. Play *piano* at measure 9 with a *crescendo* beginning in measure 13. Add a *ritardando* in measure 15 and end *mezzo forte.*

No. 51
Lifting at the end of two-note phrases keeps the momentum moving forward in this slow étude. Notice that these phrases are played with a *diminuendo* instead of a *crescendo* as in the mazurkas.

No. 52–53
These études, marked *Allegretto,* are equally effective played *Allegro.* Keep the sixteenth notes very even. As the melodic line ascends, add a *crescendo,* and as it descends, add a *diminuendo.* Do not *ritard* in the last measure but keep the tempo lively up to the last note.

No. 54
Keep the melodic line moving seamlessly between left hand and right hand. Adding a *crescendo* and a *diminuendo* at measure 7 will add dynamic interest. The editorial pedal will help keep a *legato* tone throughout the piece and accentuate the harmonic changes.